Integrating

Transition Planning

Into the IEP Process

Second Edition

Lynda L. West
Stephanie Corbey
Arden Boyer-Stephens
Bonnie Jones
Robert J. Miller
Mickey Sarkees-Wircenski

Developed by the Division of Career Development and Transition
A Division of The Council for Exceptional Children

Library of Congress Cataloging-in-Publication Data

Integrating transition planning into the IEP process, Second Edition / Lynda L. West
    . . . [et al.] : developed by Division on Career Development and Transition, a
    Division of the Council for Exceptional Children.
        p.   cm.
     Includes bibliographical references
     ISBN 0-86586-329-6
        1. Handicapped youth—Education—United States—Planning.
     2. Handicapped youth—Vocational education—United States—Planning.
     3. Handicapped youth—Employment—United States—Planning.
     4. Career education—United States—Planning.   5. Vocational
     guidance for the handicapped—United States—Planning.   I. West,
     Lynda A.   II. Council for Exceptional Children. Division on Career
     Development and Transition.
     371.91'0973—dc20   92-23152
                                                                          CIP

ISBN 0-86586-329-6

Copyright 1999 by The Council for Exceptional Children, 1920 Association
Drive, Reston, Virginia 20191-1589.

Stock No. P386S

Printed in the United States of America
10   9   8   7   6   5   4   3   2   1

About the Authors

Lynda L. West is Professor of Special Education, The George Washington University, Washington, DC. Stephanie Corbey is the Assistant Director of Special Education for Minneapolis, Minnesota Public Schools. Arden Boyer-Stephens is Student Services Coordinator for Columbia Area Career Center, Columbia, Missouri, Public Schools. Bonnie D. Jones is Program Specialist at the Office of Special Education and Rehabilitation Services, U.S. Department of Education, Washington, DC.* Robert J. Miller is Professor of Special Education, Minnesota State University in Mankato. Mickey Sarkees-Wircenski is Professor of Applied Technology, Training, and Development, University of North Texas, Denton.

*The views expressed in this book are those of the author as a former district transition coordinator and former state transition coordinator. No official support or endorsement by the U.S. Department of Education is intended or should be inferred.

Contents

1

Integrating Transition Planning into the IEP

The purpose of this guide is to assist educators, parents, and others involved in the transition planning process to help students with disabilities achieve a smooth transition from school to adult life. Transition personnel may include, but are not limited to, special educators, general educators, vocational and technical educators, social service workers, rehabilitation professionals, employers, postsecondary support service providers, residential support providers, medical providers, guidance counselors, mental health providers, and rehabilitation technology providers. With the enactment of the 1997 Individuals with Disabilities Education Act Amendments (Public Law 105-17), transition planning in the individualized education program (IEP) is required by law.

More than 300,000 special education students leave the security of high school behind each year. These individuals need assistance to receive the benefits of postsecondary education, employment, and full participation in social and leisure opportunities offered by their communities. The extent to which youths with disabilities succeed depends on the effectiveness of cooperative planning by schools, community service agencies, private organizations, and families. Cooperative planning addresses concerns about where persons with disabilities will live, work, recreate, and develop friendships.

Transition personnel, families, and individuals with disabilities need to focus not only on present educational needs but also on future needs. Thinking about the future will assist IEP planning teams in designing instructional programs that reflect the skills needed for targeted postschool environments in the areas of employment, living, community involvement, postsecondary education, and leisure pursuits.

This guide addresses topics that deal with the preparation of students with disabilities as they leave high school. It is the hope of the authors and the members of the Division on Career Development and Transition that the guide will help readers better understand, develop, and implement transition planning. References to *students* or *individuals* refer to students and individuals with disabilities who receive special education services.

WHAT IS TRANSITION?

On October 30, 1990, President Bush signed the legislation enacting Public Law 101-476. This legislation gave the Education for All Handicapped Children Act (P.L. 94-142) a new title, the Individuals with Disabilities Education Act (IDEA), and changed the language to use the term *disability* instead of *handicap.* Then, on June 4, 1997, President Clinton signed the reauthorization of the Individuals with Disabilities Education Act Amendments of 1997.

One of the most important changes in the law mandates that every eligible student have transition services incorporated into his or her IEP:

- Beginning at age 14, and updated annually, a statement of the transition service needs of the child under the applicable components of the child's IEP that focuses on the child's courses of study (such as participation in advanced-placement courses or a vocational and technical education program).

- Beginning at age 16 (or younger, if determined appropriate by the IEP Team), a statement of needed transition services for the child, including, when appropriate, a statement of the interagency responsibilities or any needed linkages.

- Beginning at least 1 year before the child reaches the age of majority under state law, a statement that the child has been informed of his or her rights under this title, if any, that will transfer to the child on reaching the age of majority.

- Students with disabilities who have graduated from high school but who have not been awarded a regular high school diploma may continue to receive special education services.

The law provides an additional mandate that says:

If a participating agency, other than the local educational agency, fails to provide the transition services described in the IEP, the local educational agency shall reconvene the IEP team to identify alternative strategies to meet the transition objectives for the child set out in that program.

The IDEA defines transition services as follows:

A coordinated set of activities for a student with a disability that—

- Is designed within an outcome-oriented process, which promotes movement from school to postschool activities, including postsecondary education, vocational training, integrated employment (including supported employment), continuing and adult education, adult services, independent living, or community participation.

- Is based upon the individual student's needs, taking into account the student's preferences and interests.

- Includes instruction, related services, community experiences, the development of employment and other postschool adult living objectives, and, when appropriate, acquisition of daily living skills and functional vocational evaluation.

WHAT IS TRANSITION PLANNING?

Transition planning is a partnership involving students with disabilities, their families, school and postschool service personnel, local community representatives, employers, and neighbors. Its purposes are to help the student choose a living situation and to ensure that the student graduates with community living skills and can access postsecondary education if that is a desired outcome. Because young people with disabilities have different levels of impairments and capabilities, transition planning needs to be flexible to meet a variety of needs. Such planning begins early, with the expectation that students have opportunities and experiences during their school years to prepare them for postschool environments as well as time to redesign strategies along the way.

To be effective, transition planning should be an intrinsic component of the student's IEP. Progressive schools provide a curriculum that prepares students for the changes and demands of life after high school. Such innovative programs offer skills instruction in natural (rather than simulated) environments, including the home; work places; and such community sites as grocery stores, offices, and restaurants.

The years of transition from school to adulthood are difficult for everyone, but especially for young people with disabilities. They leave the structured environment of school and go out into the community to face its maze of public and private agencies, which often have long waiting lists for services with different eligibility criteria. The most effective transition planning involves consumers and parents as leaders in mapping the educational experience and the years after graduation. Empowering the student and the family to do their own case management, become involved in policy-making bodies, and contribute as equal partners in the IEP process is paramount to successful transition outcomes.

Public policy has given students with disabilities and the educators who serve them a clear message regarding transition from school to work. In addition to IDEA, two laws supporting transition are in place: Public Law 105-332, the Carl D. Perkins Vocational and Applied Technology Education Act, and Public Law 100-336, the Americans with Disabilities Act. Each of these laws gives additional strength and direction regarding the design of transition programs and support services.

WHO SHOULD BE INVOLVED IN TRANSITION PLANNING?

Prior to convening the IEP meeting, careful thought should be given to who is needed to determine transition services and develop a plan to address student needs:

- Student.
- Family member.
- Special education teacher.
- Vocational education instructor.

- General educator (as appropriate).
- Special education administrator or designee.
- Community service representative(s) (e.g., community college, rehabilitation, mental health, etc.).
- Other school staff (e.g., counselor, psychologist, etc.).

These individuals can collaborate to develop a well-thought-out plan. The IEP team can then designate leadership, responsibility, targets, and timelines for proposed transition activities.

WHY IS RELATED LEGISLATION IMPORTANT TO TRANSITION?

The Carl D. Perkins Vocational and Applied Technology Education Act, which was reauthorized in 1998, and the Americans with Disabilities Act provide some important guarantees for transition services for students with disabilities. It is important for special educators to familiarize themselves with additional legislative information to be better prepared to design transition services for students with disabilities during IEP meetings.

The Workforce Investment Act of 1998 (P.L. 105-220) merged job training, adult education, and vocational rehabilitation programs into a single piece of legislation. It provides an additional opportunity to strengthen transition services. Advocates strongly hope that the independent living movement, in concert with the Americans with Disabilities Act, will strengthen consumer control over services, integrated community-based living arrangements, social change, and service based on peer relationships rather than professional-to-client relationships. In preparation for this change, teachers and families must prepare students for self-advocacy.

Understanding related legislation is important to transition planning because it helps educators prepare to identify and develop high-quality educational programming for students. If educators see the bigger picture and look beyond what special education professionals can do for transition efforts, then a team concept becomes a reality.

WHAT IS THE CARL D. PERKINS VOCATIONAL AND APPLIED TECHNOLOGY EDUCATION ACT?

The Carl D. Perkins Vocational and Applied Technology Act of 1998, P.L. 105-332, is legislation that seeks to develop more fully the academic, vocational, and technical skills of secondary students and postsecondary students who elect to enroll in vocational and technical education programs. Special populations are eligible to enroll in vocational and technical education programs. Special populations are defined as individuals with disabilities; individuals from economically disadvantaged families (including foster children); individuals preparing for nontraditional training and employment; single parents, including single pregnant women; displaced homemakers; and individuals with other barriers to educational achievement, including individuals with limited English proficiency.

Students with disabilities who are enrolled in vocational and technical education classes and require accommodations, modifications, or support services to participate must address vocational and technical education in the IEP by including specific goals and objectives.

States are required to include support for programs for special populations that lead to high-skill, high-wage careers, and specifically support for vocational and technical student organizations, especially with respect to efforts to increase the participation of students who are members of special populations. The law also requires that members of special populations will not be discriminated against on the basis of their status as members of special populations.

Permissible use of funds include the following activities:

- Providing career guidance and academic counseling for students participating in vocational and technical education programs.
- Providing work-related experiences, such as internships, cooperative education, school-based enterprises, entrepreneurship, and job shadowing, that are related to vocational and technical education programs.
- Acquiring and adapting equipment.
- Providing programs for special populations.
- Mentoring and support services.
- Supporting nontraditional training and employment activities that are consistent with the intent of the law.
- Providing vocational and technical education programs for adults and school dropouts to complete their secondary school education.

In addition, funds made available under this Act may be used (Sec. 325) to pay for the costs of vocational and technical education services required in an individualized education program developed pursuant to section 614 (d) of the Individuals with Disabilities Education Act and services necessary to meet Section 504 of the Rehabilitation Act of 1973 (now the Workforce Investment Act) with respect to ensuring equal access to vocational and technical education.

WHAT IS THE AMERICANS WITH DISABILITIES ACT?

The Americans with Disabilities Act (ADA) guarantees equal access for individuals with disabilities in the following areas:

1. Employment.

2. Public accommodations.

3. State and local government services.

4. Transportation.

5. Telecommunications.

According to the law, the individual with disabilities must be able to perform "essential functions" of the job, and an employer may not discriminate against qualified individuals. The employer is required to make "reasonable accommodations" for employees with disabilities. *Reasonable accommodation* is defined as an accommodation that does not place "undue hardship" on employers. It is important that students be aware of their rights under this law. Personnel need to be educated about ADA so they can pass this information along to individuals with whom they work (Barnes, 1991).

All state and local government facilities, services, communications, and transportation (buses, trains, subways, and other forms of transportation) must be accessible to individuals with disabilities. In addition, all places of public accommodation such as restaurants, theaters, schools, museums, and hotels must be readily accessible or the removal of barriers must be "readily achievable." *Telecommunications* refers to public telephone services, which must make accommodations for individuals with hearing and/or speech impairments to improve communication with employers and public services for individuals with disabilities.

Transition and Self-Advocacy

WHAT IS SELF-ADVOCACY?

Developing self-knowledge is the first step in attaining self-advocacy skills. Learning about one's self involves the identification of learning styles, strengths and weaknesses, interests, and preferences. For students with mild disabilities, developing an awareness of the accommodations they need will help them ask for necessary accommodations on a job and in postsecondary education. Students can also help identify alternative ways they can learn. Self-advocacy refers to:

> an individual's ability to effectively communicate, convey, negotiate or assert his or her own interests, desires, needs, and rights. It involves making informed decisions and taking responsibility for those decisions. (VanReusen et al., 1994)

Self-advocacy is not a new concept in disability services. Enabling and empowering students to direct their own lives has been an underpinning of federal legislation for some time. For example, the Workforce Investment Act of 1998, Title I, Vocational Rehabilitation Program, describes the philosophy of independent living as including consumer control, peer support, self-help, self-determination, equal access, and individual and system advocacy, in order to maximize the leadership empowerment, independence, and productivity of persons with disabilities.

HOW CAN WE IMPROVE SELF-ADVOCACY?

There are many components in developing self-advocacy skills in young adults who are engaged in the transition process. Helping the student to identify future goals or desired outcomes in transition planning areas is a good place to begin. Self-awareness/self-knowledge is critical for the student in determining the direction that transition planning will take.

Many tools and resources are available to assist transition planning teams in conducting a student-centered planning approach (see resource section). The following sections provide some additional strategies to help individuals with disabilities develop self-advocacy skills.

Promote the Student as a Self-Advocate

Encourage the student to be active in the IEP process and other decision-making situations. Assist the student in compiling and developing an exit file. This file should include the last IEP, a transition plan, documentation of disability, recent test scores and assessment summaries, a list of strengths and areas of need, a list of home or work accommodations needed, a summary of learning style, letters of recommendation, and the telephone numbers of service providers. This file empowers the student and encourages self-knowledge. Self-advocacy issues and lessons will be most effective if they are integrated daily.

Respond to Students Who Self-Advocate Appropriately

Listen to the problem and ask the student for input on possible accommodations or modifications that he or she may need. Talk with the student about possible solutions, discussing the positive and negative sides. A person who self-advocates should not feel alone. Good self-advocates know how to ask questions and get help from other people. They do not let other people do everything for them or tell them what to do. Self-advocates are assertive. Assertive people tell others what they want and need, but they do not demand things. They respect the rights and feelings of other people. They talk over their ideas with other people. They ask questions for guidance, then make up their own minds after reviewing the information. They may have strong feelings, but they try to be objective when making their decisions.

Identify Strategies for Teaching Self-Advocacy

Students need opportunities to practice newly acquired self-advocacy skills. Teachers may wish to have students role play various situations in which they can practice skills such as the following:

- Setting up a class schedule.
- Moving out of the home.
- Asking for accommodations needed for a course.
- Meeting with a rehabilitation counselor or social service caseworker.
- Meeting with a medical provider.
- Working with a personal care attendant.
- Interviewing for a job.
- Making choices in an IEP meeting.

Students apply self-advocacy skills by calling and requesting information about a service they need for transition from high school. Students can prepare to visit an adult service provider by compiling a list of questions to ask and requests for services.

Identify Examples of Self-Advocacy Objectives on an IEP

Following are some examples of objectives for an IEP that would promote development of self-advocacy. Students will:

- State their rights as mandated under the Individuals with Disabilities Act Amendments of 1997, P.L. 105-17.
- State their rights as mandated under Title I of the Workforce Investment Act of 1998 (Vocational Rehabilitation) and Americans with Disabilities Act (ADA).
- Be able to access information from the support service staff of the postsecondary school in which they have expressed an interest.
- State the type of information necessary to self-advocate.
- Define the terms *assertive, passive,* and *aggressive.*
- Identify assertive, passive, and aggressive behavior in written scenarios.
- State examples of their own assertive, passive, and aggressive behaviors.
- Respond assertively in a given situation.

Identify Student Skills Needed for Self-Advocacy in a Job Interview

Students need specific self-advocacy skills for job interviews. Here are a few examples:

- Be prepared: Complete an application and a résumé.
- Be alert: Greet interviewer, establish eye contact, and sit up straight.
- Be an interested listener: Show enthusiasm.
- Express yourself clearly: Avoid slang and negative comments.
- Tell about yourself: Describe your strengths, goals, and past experiences.
- Ask questions: Show interest and energy.
- Describe what you have to offer or the types of work you want to do: Demonstrate self-confidence and enthusiasm.

These are just a few examples of the techniques educators and parents can use to ensure that students have the self-advocacy skills needed to make the transition from school to work. It is important that self-advocacy be recognized as a critical component of transition if the ultimate goal of transition—independence—is to be achieved.

WHY IS SELF-ADVOCACY PART OF TRANSITION?

No one has a greater stake in the outcome of transition planning than the student with a disability. The student should be an active, participating member of the transition team, as well as the focus of all activities. For a young person with a disability, decision making is complicated by limited choices and the tendency for others to tell the individual what to do.

Too often students are taught that dependence, passivity, and reliance on unseen forces will take care of them. Throughout transition planning, students should be encouraged to express concerns, preferences, and conclusions about their options and to give facts and reasons. They may need to learn how to express their thoughts in a way that makes others listen to them and respect their views. In order to learn these skills, students need to practice them within a supportive environment. The transition process is a good place to start. Transition planning should be an ongoing opportunity for students to learn and practice responsibility and self-knowledge. Transition is an ever-changing process, and students need to be skillful enough to adapt to the challenge of those changes.

WHAT ARE A STUDENT'S RIGHTS AND RESPONSIBILITIES AT THE IEP MEETING?

Paulson and O'Leary (1991) have expressed their belief that part of the IEP planning process for educators is preparing the student for participation in the IEP meeting. Educators need to stress the importance of attendance at the IEP meeting and encourage the student to take an active part. The student has the right to (a) be at the IEP meeting, (b) give his or her opinion, and (c) have the objectives he or she wants included in the IEP meeting.

In return, the student's responsibilities include:

- Thinking about what he or she wants for the future.
- Communicating with parents and teachers to determine realistic goals.
- Sharing feelings with the IEP team.
- Following up on objectives for which he or she is responsible.

In order to carry out the full intent of federal legislation, ample opportunities must be provided for students to take an active, participatory role in the transition planning process. The IEP meeting is the critical moment when opportunities for participation are duly noted by all team members.

3

Identification of Needs and Assessment

Assessment of students with disabilities can take many forms, depending on the information needed for planning and instruction. Both short-range and long-range planning should begin early. Assessment is ongoing throughout a student's school career. Beginning as early as kindergarten, the IEP should contain career and prevocational goals and objectives. By the time a student reaches the middle school or junior high level, assessment will become more systematized and focused on transition to adult roles.

WHAT IS ASSESSMENT?

Assessment is a process of compiling information already available on a student into a profile to determine the student's current status in a variety of areas. A review of the student's permanent record, past IEPs and diagnostic summaries, classroom observations, and informal interviews with the student and parents can produce an abundance of information. A school guidance counselor may also have a portfolio of skills mastered by the student. A summary of this information can help teachers, parents, and students make decisions about curriculum needs and IEP goals and objectives.

WHO CONDUCTS ASSESSMENT?

Most school districts have counselors who help students define their future goals. Some schools have a guidance curriculum that defines developmental tasks for students. Counselors are a vital resource when assessing a student's strengths and weaknesses in a variety of adult roles. They can administer assessment instruments, and many have a portfolio on each student that records mastery of developmental tasks in such areas as career development, personal–social skills, independent living skills, and decision-making skills. Counselors, however, are not the only personnel who have a major responsibility in the assessment of students for transition planning. All educators, the student, parents, employers, and friends can contribute valuable information to transition planning in the IEP process.

WHAT TYPES OF INFORMATION ARE COLLECTED?

There are many areas to consider when planning for a student's transition. Readiness for independent living and vocational skills should be addressed in each evaluation of a student for special education services. Sarkees-Wircenski and Scott (1995) have provided a list of areas assessment should cover, including:

- Basic skills.
- Communication skills.
- Ability to follow directions.
- Coordination.
- Self-confidence.
- Personal hygiene and grooming.
- Ability to work with others.
- Work habits.
- Preferred learning style. (p. 106)

WHAT ARE THE METHODS OF COLLECTING DATA?

Observation checklists can provide a wealth of information about the student. It may be helpful to have parents, teachers, employers, and peers complete the checklists so that a full picture of the student emerges. It is also recommended that the student use these informal measures for self-evaluation. Realistic self-evaluation is a skill all students should possess, and practice will develop these skills. A comparison of the student's self-evaluation and others' evaluations can often provide the student with a more realistic appraisal of skills and behaviors.

Systematic observation of students in various environments is also a valuable tool to gather functional assessment information. Sometimes a formal vocational evaluation may be beneficial to help the student plan for career goals.

HOW IS ASSESSMENT USED?

Assessment information must be organized and profiled carefully to reveal patterns in the student's vocational development and directions for future vocational programming and transition planning. If students, parents, or teachers disagree on goals for the student or testing indicates needs that might prevent a student from reaching stated goals, assessment of a more formal nature may need to be pursued. This assessment would concentrate on areas of discrepancy, which would help planners come to a consensus.

WHO COLLECTS ASSESSMENT DATA?

Teachers, parents, and students can furnish information related to the student's interests, skills, and special needs based on behavior observations, interviews, and stated desires. What the student wants to do as an adult and what the parent wants the student to do can be good indicators for planning an educational program. Together, teachers, parents, and the student can make good judgments about the student's skills and abilities and can help plan for any special instruction or accommodations that might be needed. Special instruction might include various curriculum options such as community-based instruction, a work experience program, vocational and technical education classes, or academic preparation for entry into college. The special needs might include the student's need for different teaching methods according to his or her learning style, needs for interagency cooperation to provide work experience, use of assistive technology, or transportation needs for program implementation.

WHAT IS CURRICULUM-BASED ASSESSMENT?

One practical and functional approach to vocational assessment is the use of assessment procedures that are linked to the curricula. Curriculum-based vocational assessment (CBVA) involves the identification of an individual's career or vocational strengths and weaknesses for purposes of making decisions that will affect programming and instruction (Stodden, Ianacone, Boone, & Bisconer, 1987). The primary strength of CBVA is its direct relevance to existing curricula and its direct applicability to ongoing curriculum and instructional activities within a variety of settings.

The CBVA can be applied in a variety of settings. The process is designed to be molded by the unique characteristics and resources of any system that needs to collect performance-based information to assist in making programming and placement decisions. For instance, the CBVA process is structured to accommodate and specifically address the purpose, intent, resources, and personnel available within a system (e.g., school, adult service, rehabilitation, or direct employment site). The fundamental premise of the process is that useful vocational assessment information can be obtained by effectively using the resources and environments available within one's setting. The unique features of the CBVA can best be realized by:

1. Structuring information and performance-based evaluation activities within a career/vocational framework.

2. Collecting and compiling this information over time in a variety of environments.

3. Formalizing the evaluation, synthesis, and application process to obtain the most complete picture of the student, client, or worker.

Depending on the system, the availability of assessment environments will vary, as will their direct relationship to vocational and employment settings. Regardless of this relationship, information extracted from academic, vocational, or functional living curricula can provide valuable information on work-related behaviors, functional skills, interests, and aptitudes.

WHAT IS FUNCTIONAL BEHAVIORAL ASSESSMENT?

Functional behavioral assessment uses systematic observation in various environments and a multidisciplinary team to identify the "function" of the behavior; that is, *why* the student is using the behavior or what benefits the student receives from the behavior. This becomes important also in determining whether the behavior is a part of the student's disability (for disciplinary purposes). Gathering data regarding behavior can be time consuming, as it requires systematic observations in different environments. Students should be observed in each of their classes, using the same observation checklist. Parents might be asked to use the checklist at home during various times of the day. When analyzing the data gathered (called *baseline data*), patterns will emerge that indicate types of environments/situations where the challenging behavior(s) is manifested. Once these environments/situations are identified, one or two might be chosen to develop a management plan.

WHAT IS FORMAL ASSESSMENT?

Assessment can be divided into three levels (Maxam, 1985). A Level I assessment is informal and consists of reviewing and compiling existing data on an individual student. Level II assessments are performed when the Level I data are insufficient to make decisions about future goals. More data are gathered, often using standardized test batteries to obtain information on interests and aptitudes. A Level III assessment is referred to as a *comprehensive vocational assessment* or *vocational evaluation* and is performed when the data produced by Levels I and II are inconclusive for program planning.

Formal assessment is usually performed by personnel who are trained in the area of assessment. For a Level II assessment, a qualified school counselor might administer an interest inventory or aptitude test. This additional information may be enough for the planning team to make decisions for the vocational preparation of the student. If the Level II data do not provide enough information to make a decision, a comprehensive vocational evaluation would be recommended.

Level III assessment, or comprehensive vocational evaluation, is performed by personnel trained in this specialty area. Various standardized and criterion-referenced instruments are administered to the student, including interest tests, aptitude tests, and hands-on work samples (portions of real jobs). The vocational evaluator is also trained in behavior observation. He or she writes an evaluation report that includes behaviors pertinent to instruction or work (such as interpersonal skills, organizational skills in relation to tasks, etc.). Not all school districts have access to a formal vocational evaluation unit.

Formal vocational evaluation units are useful to help students make decisions about their interests and abilities. Students are exposed to a variety of real job tasks so that they can make better decisions about whether or not they like doing the task. Some students find that the jobs they thought they would like require too much reading or writing, and they change their goals to more realistic career options. The written reports from a comprehensive vocational evaluation can provide a wealth of information upon which to base decisions for both short-range and long-range goals.

For students with severe disabilities, a community-based vocational evaluation may provide better data than a traditional comprehensive vocational evaluation (Browder, 1987). Many of the work samples in a comprehensive vocational evaluation center may be related to jobs that students with severe limitations would be unable to perform. For all students, especially students with severe disabilities, an assessment in the community might yield more useful data (Halpern & Fuhrer, 1984). Student interest is assessed informally, and potential jobs in the community that are related to their interests are identified. These jobs are task analyzed and taught to students in the environment in which the jobs are found (in the factory, grocery store, etc.). A task analysis is fairly easy to do. It consists of the following steps:

1. Watch the task being done.

2. Do the task yourself until you are proficient.

3. Write down each step of the task in behavioral terms.

4. Do the task again, following your written directions.

5. Have someone who is familiar with the task follow your directions.

6. Correct errors on the written directions.

7. Have someone who is unfamiliar with the task perform it from the written directions.

8. Correct any unclear directions.

A student is instructed in the task, and his or her performance is recorded on each job assessed. Allowing students to be instructed in two or three different jobs exposes them to other potential interest areas and increases their ability to make decisions about what kind of work they want to do.

Special educators have long used assessment tools to establish eligibility for services, program placement, development of IEP goals and objectives, and monitoring progress toward goals. Some of the assessment tools are standardized (e.g., intelligence tests), but many are informal tools such as observation, questionnaires, and frequency counts (Guerin & Maier, 1983). With the need for planning for the transition of students, these tools ought to become even more helpful. Special educators who include vocational readiness and vocational information routinely in their diagnostic and yearly assessments will have more information upon which to plan for transition. Recent research literature cautions against overreliance on standardized testing unless it is used in conjunction with informal methods.

Vocational assessment information is very useful to help determine appropriate vocational program placement of individuals with disabilities. This assessment may be informal or formal, depending on the information needed for decision making. A vocational assessment can provide direction for the placement decision as well as delineate the special needs of the student in regard to delivery of instruction (teaching methods), testing accommodations, and support services needed for success (Meers, 1987).

Special educators must make a concerted effort to improve and summarize assessment information and share it with vocational rehabilitation or adult service providers. Collaboration in the use of assessment data by all transition team members will ensure cost effectiveness and minimize duplication for students and consumers. It is an important step in the referral process. Some students with disabilities will be referred to Vocational Rehabilitation for services during their high school years. A comprehensive vocational evaluation can sometimes be purchased by Vocational Rehabilitation during the student's secondary education. Having results available to Vocational Rehabilitation counselors can decrease the referral or eligibility time for students and help the counselors make decisions with students about their future goals.

For students who may be referred to the Department of Mental Health or to the Department of Mental Retardation/Developmental Disabilities for services after school completion, the vocational evaluation results will also be helpful for planning. In all cases, the evaluation results will reduce the amount of time needed for adult agencies to assess transition services.

For students who plan postsecondary education in some form, special attention should be paid to the type of assessment documentation necessary for accommodations in the postsecondary setting. For example, students with learning disabilities may need a traditional standardized reevaluation prior to graduation.

Adult service agencies should be a part of the transition planning for students with disabilities. In most cases, this means being a part of the IEP team early in the high school program. Agency personnel will have questions about the student that can be answered through appropriate vocational assessment. Be sure to include these personnel in the planning for assessment of students. This will save them time and money and save the student from undergoing another assessment after completion of high school. Future plans and goals will already have been determined, and the adult service agency already will have been informed as to the interests, abilities, and special needs of the young adult entering their service domain.

Individual Planning for Transition

The transition planning process is driven through the development of the IEP. The IEP consists of an annual planning document listing goals and objectives to be mastered for the year. In order to incorporate transition into the IEP, all goals and objectives must be selected based on current levels of performance and anticipated future environments.

The IEP must address transition needs starting at age 14, or earlier when appropriate. It is recognized that career development is a lifelong process that begins as a student enters elementary school; as such, the IEPs of all students, regardless of age or intent, do address the needs of future environments. The IEP integrates the transition plan by using the following components:

- Descriptions of abilities and limitations as they relate to present and future needs.

- Collaboration between school personnel such as vocational educators, special educators, guidance counselors, general educators, and nurses.

- Coordination with community and adult service providers and postsecondary institutions as contributors of information and resources.

- Involvement of parents and students as active participants in the planning process.

To integrate students with disabilities into school and community settings, IEP goals should focus on the least restrictive environments for skill acquisition. In many cases the community is the only suitable environment for learning transition skills.

Anticipation of adult environments that the student will be functioning in, and provision of cumulative annual IEPs, prepare the student to make the transition to the adult environment. An effective transition occurs when the student has the necessary skills and supports in place to be successful in the adult environment.

The IEP team meeting is vital to the coordination and development of transition. The IEP manager must gather a team that includes the participants needed to fulfill the needs of the student. If IEP team members from the community and service agencies or postsecondary institutions are not available to attend the IEP planning meeting in person, it is important to have their input and information available for consideration at the meeting.

HOW ARE FUTURE GOALS INCORPORATED INTO THE IEP?

Anticipated adult environments are targeted as future goals (transition outcomes) based on assessment data, IEP team input, family values and resources, and student preferences. When future goals are selected, some considerations may include medical needs, transportation, individual strengths and limitations, necessary support services, degree of occupational skill development, jobs available in the community, community resources, and recreation and leisure opportunities. Future goals should be based not on what is currently available in the community but on the needs and desires of the individual and family involved. Resources and services can be developed to meet the desired future goals.

Adult environments fall into the domains of postsecondary training and learning: jobs and job training, home living, community participation, and recreation and leisure skills. Curriculum and resources are available for each domain. What is important is that the comprehensive needs of the student be matched to the appropriate curriculum in order to achieve desired future goals.

IEP team members are responsible for ensuring that the student acquires the necessary skills to reach the anticipated future goals when the transition is complete. This means that the IEP team must know what skills will be required for the student to be successful in the targeted adult environment. Skills may include the following, among others:

- Job seeking and retention skills.
- Specific occupational skills.
- Generalizable skills such as reading, computation, writing, communication, problem solving, note taking, critical thinking, and decision making.
- Social skills.
- Self-advocacy skills.
- Community functional skills such as transportation.
- Home living skills such as cooking.

Curriculum, instruction, experience, and other avenues provide opportunities for the student to acquire the needed skills. The IEP team should look to such avenues as general education, vocational and technical education, special education, community experiences, and home experiences for the acquisition of skills. Services and supports can come from community organizations, agencies, guidance and career counselors, special educators, job placement specialists, peers, and family members.

WHAT ARE THE ROLES AND RESPONSIBILITIES OF IEP TEAM MEMBERS IN PLANNING?

A cooperative effort will be required by a variety of agencies and individuals if the IEP is to become a successful vehicle for preparing individuals with disabilities for employment and independent living. The primary responsibility of the IEP team should be to develop, implement, and evaluate the IEP as well as to see that necessary resources and support services are provided so that transition activities will be successful.

Team members involved in developing and implementing the IEP could include the following:

1. *The Student.* The student assumes responsibility for identifying a career path, suggesting activities and services for his or her own transition plan, and providing feedback about the quality of experiences and services provided. The student states preferences and desires as well as committing to the plan. The student should be actively involved in the IEP process, and if the student has been well trained in the self-directed IEP process, then he or she should lead the meeting.

2. *Parents and Family.* Family members participate in all phases of the IEP development, implementation, and evaluation. They provide valuable feedback to other team members. They provide insight into the background and needs of the student. They also actively participate in and reinforce IEP activities as well as serving in an advocacy role.

3. *Special Education Personnel.* These educators assist in collecting information necessary to establish IEP goals and objectives with the student, coordinate services and resources, provide direct instruction and reinforcement to the student, and help match student needs and interests with an appropriate career path. It is critical that they coordinate the activities in the IEP from one level to the next (e.g., facilitate the student's movement from elementary to middle school, middle school to high school) to provide a smooth and comprehensive transition within the school-based program and beyond.

4. *Administrators.* Administrators promote a positive attitude toward transition programming as it is developed through the IEP and provide the resources needed to implement IEP activities and services.

5. *Vocational Instructors.* Vocational personnel help provide the student with career development experiences and specific vocational instruction. They identify instructional and placement sites in the local community and recommend necessary supports.

6. *Teachers.* Regular education teachers teach and reinforce skills in the general education curriculum that are necessary to the career path chosen by the student. Regular education teachers are required to be included in the IEP team meeting if the student is, or may be, participating in the regular education environment. They must, to the extent appropriate, participate in the develop-

ment, review, and revision of the student's IEP. They assist in determining positive behavioral interventions, supplementary aids and services, program modifications, or supports for school personnel.

7. *Guidance Counselors.* Guidance personnel provide career and personal development information, conduct and interpret career assessment activities, and help coordinate support services documented in the IEP. They monitor the diploma and graduation requirements.

8. *School Support Personnel.* Support personnel represent a variety of diverse backgrounds and expertise that can be used to implement the activities documented in the IEP (e.g., remedial academic instructors, resource personnel, psychologists, speech therapists, occupational/physical therapists, personal care attendants, job coaches).

9. *Service Agencies and Adult Service Providers.* Representatives of agencies and adult service providers present specific information to the team regarding the type and kind of services available through the agency; requirements to qualify for services; availability of services at the local level; procedures for applications; and contact person, location, and telephone number. Examples of agencies and adult services providers include the following:

   - Vocational Rehabilitation Services.
   - Department of Mental Health/Mental Retardation.
   - Commission for the Blind.
   - Division for the Hearing Impaired.
   - Department of Human Services.
   - State Employment Commission.

10. *Postsecondary Education Personnel.* Postsecondary education representatives provide information about available instructional programs, admission requirements and procedures, support services provided to students with disabilities, and articulation strategies that have been coordinated with secondary programs.

11. *Employers and Members of the Business Community.* These individuals provide valuable information concerning the labor needs of business and industry, changes in technology and the impact on instructional programs and curricula, and current and future job prospects. They can also provide instructional sites and participate in transition activities (e.g., job shadowing, guest speakers, job fairs).

12. *Work Experience Coordinators.* These individuals are school-based educators whose primary responsibilities include developing job sites, setting up supports, placing students in work sites, supervising student progress, and acting as liaisons between school programs and employers.

13. *Transition Specialists.* These individuals provide the liaison between the school, the home, and various adult service providers who are assisting the student in the transition process. Their roles and responsibilities are as diverse as the students they serve.

While all of these transition team members may not be involved at the same time, teachers, other professionals, and families should look to every source available for assistance. It is important to remember that transition planning is not an exact science but an art. Together, the team members must ask themselves a series of questions to help guide the transition planning process. Following are some examples of questions that must be addressed by the IEP team:

1. Which agency or individual assumes what type of responsibility for a specific student?

2. When does each transition activity or service begin and how long should it last?

3. What criteria should be used to determine whether or not the planning documented in the IEP has been executed successfully?

5

Curriculum for Successful Transition

A full generation of students with disabilities has moved through the public education system since P.L. 94-142 was enacted in 1975. During this time, researchers have suggested and practitioners have implemented a variety of instructional approaches, delivery models, and programs designed to provide for the unique educational needs of students in special education. As students with disabilities emerged from the school system into work and adult living, national attention began to focus on this first generation of individuals to benefit from the legislation.

If students do not achieve the expected postschool outcomes, the IEP team must seriously examine instructional content for each student, especially at the secondary school level. In recent years, researchers have suggested that changes in curriculum are necessary if students are to attain a significant improvement in postschool adjustment and quality of life (Edgar, 1987; Halpern & Benz, 1987). Two major changes are recommended:

- Provide for basic academic skill instruction along with functional or life skills instruction.

- Teach functional and life skills in natural settings (home, school, community, work).

Students must be able to function both in and outside of the classroom.

WHAT IS FUNCTIONAL CURRICULUM?

Clark (1990) defined functional curriculum as "instructional content that focuses on the concepts and skills needed by students . . . in order to achieve life adjustment. These concepts and skills are individually determined through functional assessment and are targeted for current and future needs" (p. 3). Just as academic skills are taught in a logical scope and sequence, functional or life skills can be organized in a curriculum as well. The idea, however, is not to have two separate curricula, but to have a continuum unique to the current needs and postsecondary goals of the student.

To help the student achieve a successful adjustment after high school, the curriculum must be linked to the skills the student will need. General education students participate in a college preparatory curriculum if they expect to enroll in a community college or university program after high school. Likewise, other students may participate in a technical/vocational curriculum if they plan to enter a community college, a university, a vocational school, an apprenticeship program, or employment in the workforce. Students with special needs and their families must also target postsecondary goals by age 16 or earlier. The next step, then, is for the IEP team to select or develop a curriculum that includes skills that are important for success in the identified postschool environment.

Halpern (1985) identified three major environments or domains of adjustment for the postschool years: personal–social networks, daily living, and employment. A comprehensive functional curriculum includes life skills in all three environments or domains. A good example of a comprehensive functional curriculum is the Life-Centered Career Education Curriculum (LCCE) (Brolin, 1997). LCCE divides three broad categories into a number of skills and subskills identified as important for successful adjustment in adult life.

WHAT ARE DAILY LIVING SKILLS?

Daily living skills, sometimes referred to as *independent living skills*, are the skills required to function independently or within a family environment. People with good daily living skills become responsible adults within home, school, community, and work environments. Daily living skills instruction is the responsibility not only of special education teachers, but also of parents, general education teachers, and even peers. The following are some examples of these skills:

- Managing personal finances.
- Selecting and managing a household.
- Caring for personal needs.
- Being aware of safety.
- Raising, preparing, and consuming food.
- Buying and caring for clothing.
- Exhibiting responsible citizenship.
- Using recreational facilities and engaging in leisure activities.
- Getting around the community. (Brolin, 1982, 1989, 1997)

WHAT ARE PERSONAL AND SOCIAL SKILLS?

Personal and social skills are closely linked with a satisfying adult life. However, peer relations and social learning are a common problem for students with disabilities. Inappropriate personal and social skills are frequently noted by employers as a reason for job termination (Rusch & Chadsey-Rusch, 1985).

Problem-solving, decision-making, and self-advocacy skills are especially critical in this category (Ianacone & Stodden, 1985). LCCE skills in this domain include:

- Achieving self-awareness.
- Acquiring self-confidence.
- Achieving socially responsible behavior.
- Maintaining good interpersonal skills.
- Achieving independence.
- Achieving problem-solving skills.
- Communicating with others.

WHAT ARE OCCUPATIONAL SKILLS?

Work is the fundamental activity of adult life. Society values and rewards workers through wages, benefits, labor laws, and recognition as an employee or worker. Given the large unemployment and underemployment rates among persons with disabilities, a heavy emphasis on career and vocational preparation is appropriate for any student who expects to enter the workforce. LCCE's occupational guidance and preparation category includes the following skills:

- Knowing and exploring occupational options.
- Selecting and planning occupational choices.
- Exhibiting appropriate work habits and behavior.
- Seeking, securing, and maintaining employment.
- Exhibiting sufficient physical and manual skills.
- Obtaining specific occupational skills.

For students who participate in vocational, career, and/or technical education, these skills would be integrated into their curriculum and could be reinforced by support personnel and/or special education teachers.

HOW CAN A FUNCTIONAL CURRICULUM
BE INDIVIDUALIZED?

Although educators usually consider the LCCE curriculum and its implementation strategies appropriate for students with mild to moderate disabilities, the daily living skills, personal and social skills, and occupational skills domains are equally appropriate for *all* students, regardless of disability. The subskills under each domain are analyzed to a greater degree to reflect the needs of the student more adequately.

For a completely individualized approach to identifying functional skills, Wehman, Moon, Everson, Wood, and Barcus (1988) have suggested that teachers and other IEP team members use a process called *ecological analysis*, which includes the following steps:

1. Select a major curricular domain for analysis (daily living skills, personal and social skills, or occupational skills).

2. Identify environments or settings for the selected domains (home, school, community, workplace). Include environments identified by the students, parents, and other IEP team members.

3. Observe the environments and record the skills that are necessary to function within the identified environments.

4. Check the targeted skills with the parents and other IEP team members to assure accuracy.

5. Repeat Steps 1 through 4 with the other two domains.

6. Review the results periodically and revise as necessary.

This process requires time spent in other environments outside the school and therefore requires administrative support.

WHAT DOES IT MEAN TO TEACH IN NATURAL SETTINGS?

A key principle and instructional strategy associated with functional curriculum is the notion of teaching in natural settings. This means that teaching takes place in the environment in which the skill is naturally employed. For example, "sorting laundry" occurs in a home setting; "making a bank deposit" occurs in the community; and "participating in a consumer math class" occurs at school. For secondary students, job training occurs at a real workplace in the community, rather than in a simulated work environment or sheltered workshop. On the other hand, many functional skills are appropriately taught in all settings. For example, problem-solving skills from the personal and social skills category are important not only in the home, school, and community, but also at work. Likewise, safety awareness, from the daily living skills category, is needed in the home, workplace, and community setting. Furthermore, learning in natural settings allows students with disabilities to experience associations and natural interactions with nondisabled community members. Balance is needed so students are not isolated from the community or their peers at school.

WHAT IS THE RELATIONSHIP BETWEEN TRANSITION AND FUNCTIONAL CURRICULUM?

The school-to-adult life transition is a process that can be defined by many characteristics. Functional curriculum is at the core of transition activities during the school years. Rusch and DeStefano (1989) have identified common strategies or characteristics among successful secondary school transition programs. The framework of these strategies provides the foundation for successful student transition:

(1) Early planning.

(2) Collaborative team of decision makers for identifying support services.

(3) An individualized transition plan.

(4) Instruction in natural, integrated settings.

(5) Community-based training.

(6) Functional curriculum.

(7) Job development using family and local business resources.

(8) Job placement prior to graduation.

(9) Ongoing staff development.

(10) Program evaluation activities. (pp. 1–2)

WHEN SHOULD A FUNCTIONAL CURRICULUM APPROACH BE USED?

Although functional curriculum can be started at any time, experts recommend that a functional curriculum be used from the elementary school years (Boyer-Stephens & Kearns, 1988; West, 1987). In this way, a student's IEP will

- Target identified functional and academic skills in an integrated plan.
- Help maximize student growth throughout the school years in all domains.
- Facilitate a smooth transition to postsecondary environments.

IEP team members must ask the following questions about each skill:

- Is it appropriate to the student's age peers?
- Is it a skill needed to function independently within the student's local community?
- Is it based on the student's current needs? On postsecondary goals or plans?
- Do the parents or other family members think the skill is important?
- Have we considered all domains? All environments within each domain?
- What is the natural setting for this skill?
- Are student preferences considered?

6

Support Services

About half of the youths in this country receive little assistance in pursuing post-secondary education or in making the transition from school to employment. Many individuals flounder in the labor force after leaving school, either obtaining jobs with few opportunities for advancement or remaining unemployed (Sarkees-Wircenski & Scott, 1995).

The educational system plays an important role in an ongoing process of preparing individuals for a life of work and learning. The educational experience should provide a solid foundation of skills and knowledge that will prepare individuals for meaningful employment and continuing education. The attention of all educators should be focused on assessing the unique needs of individual students, establishing learning environments that support learner needs, teaching skills and knowledge that have a direct bearing on life after high school, and counseling students and families for a smooth transition to jobs and post-secondary education (Sarkees-Wircenski & Scott, 1995, p. 634).

No one program or technique will work for all students. Research suggests that the following concepts are beneficial in preparing individuals for the future:

1. Workforce readiness will be enhanced if exposure to career options begins in kindergarten and continues through high school.

2. Students will be better prepared for life outside of school if school activities are made more relevant to the real world.

3. Young people who do not plan to attend college are in urgent need of new or enhanced programs that develop their workplace skills and prepare them for the transition to life outside of school (Texas Education Agency Clearinghouse, 1993).

According to the mandates of IDEA, the individualized education program (IEP) developed each year for every learner must include a statement of the needed transition services beginning at age 14, as well as interagency responsibilities or linkages before the student leaves the school setting. This approach is a student-centered one, concentrating on the present and future needs of the student, not on what services are currently available.

The transition mandate requires a shift in the perspective of the IEP planning team. Rather than viewing the needs of a student on a 9- or 12-month basis, the team, including the student, must focus on long-range goals. Discussion of the long-range goals will uncover support services necessary for the next year or the next several years. In this way, plans can be made to ensure the availability of the services by the time they are needed.

To provide an effective, comprehensive system of support services, all available resources, including those in the school, the total school system, and the community, should be identified and utilized. Parents, students, business and industry representatives, school administrators, faculty, counselors, and all school staff, as well as community service providers, must work cooperatively and collaboratively.

To be effective, services must be:

- Drawn from all the resources of the school and community.

- Provided on an individual basis as needed.

- Coordinated to ensure that all students receive the necessary services.

High-quality, comprehensive, and coordinated support services can make a difference in every learner's educational and occupational future. The support services must facilitate the student's success in school and the transition beyond school. Shoultz and colleagues (1991) identified four domains that should be included in a system of support services for individuals with disabilities:

- Assessment—Students complete formal and/or informal assessments, which may include achievement, personality, interests, aptitude, or other activities to gather relevant, realistic, and accurate student information.

- Planning—Students identify an individualized academic and career goal based upon their assessment results.

- Implementation—Students should be able to access student services based on their individual needs. Examples of these services include: tutoring, counseling, career and academic advising, remedial instruction, child care assistance, and developmental education services.

- Follow-up and evaluation—The data collected determine the adherence to performance standards set by the institution, outside agencies, federal guidelines, and state requirements. Continuous data gathering and evaluation lead to the identification of system strengths and areas needing improvement. These data should be the basis for all program improvement (pp. 7–8).

WHO PROVIDES SUPPORT SERVICES
IN SECONDARY SETTINGS?

Special education maintains a continuum of service delivery, and students are placed into program areas based on their needs. The continuum may range from homebound instruction to inclusion in regular educational settings. Support services are available within each of the delivery systems.

Partners in the collaborative planning process include:

- Academic instructors and other general education teachers.
- Administrators.
- Assistive technology teachers/consultants.
- Bilingual personnel.
- Cooperative education personnel/work study coordinators.
- Cultural and religious organizations.
- Curriculum coordinators.
- Employers.
- Families.
- Interpreters, direct readers, note takers.
- Itinerant personnel.
- Job coaches.
- Media specialists.
- Nurses/medical personnel.
- Occupational therapists.
- Paraprofessionals/aides.
- Physical therapists.
- Rehabilitation services personnel.
- Remedial academic personnel.
- School guidance counselors.
- School psychologists.
- Social workers.
- Special education personnel.
- Special populations coordinators.
- Speech therapists/communication specialists.

- Students as self-advocates.
- Vocational and applied technology education personnel.
- Vocational assessment personnel.

Social workers and vocational rehabilitation counselors can provide a wealth of information that is helpful to the planning team. Social workers who are familiar with the community can assist in identifying residential services and recreational and leisure services. They may also explain the regulations surrounding Social Security benefits. This knowledge can help education personnel, parents, and the student prepare for the student's future needs. Vocational Rehabilitation counselors possess in-depth knowledge regarding careers, job requirements, and instructional opportunities, as well as the ability to provide student counseling. Vocational Rehabilitation counselors will also be familiar with the Americans with Disabilities Act and its requirements for employers and community services. This information can help build more realistic career options.

When planning for a student to enter vocational courses, the IEP team should ensure that representatives from Vocational Rehabilitation and the vocational program are present. The IEP should contain the goals for the school year and the long-range career goals of the student. The student should have ample encouragement to participate in the development of the IEP and in the designation of necessary support services.

Examples of modifications that may be necessary to meet the specific needs of learners with disabilities who enroll in a vocational program are described below. This does not mean the vocational curriculum is "watered down." Students with disabilities must have adequate backgrounds for vocational courses. The support service accommodations provided only recognize the limitations resulting from the disability and strive to circumvent those limitations.

1. *Curriculum modification.* Provide extended time for mastering the competencies for completion of the course.

2. *Equipment modification.* Install a specialized circuit board that allows for single-key commands instead of dual-key commands on computers.

3. *Classroom modification.* Provide desks or tables that are accessible to individuals using wheelchairs.

4. *Instructional aids and devices.* Allow more time for testing, read tests aloud, provide access to word processing for written work, and provide taped textbooks.

5. *Support personnel.* Make basic skills instructors, vocational assessment personnel, vocational counselors, specialized job placement personnel, paraprofessionals, tutors, and interpreters available when needed.

6. *Vocational teachers and vocational support personnel.* Work closely to ensure that students with disabilities have the necessary accommodations for success.

WHO PROVIDES SUPPORT SERVICES
IN POSTSECONDARY SETTINGS?

In the postsecondary setting, IEPs are not required. Students must be taught to be self-advocates if they desire support services. They must identify themselves to the appropriate personnel on campus and be able to identify and prove their disabilities to access accommodations. It is also helpful if students can identify and request the types of support services they need. Most postsecondary institutions do have support services available for students who request such services. Many institutions are developing specialized services for individuals with learning disabilities. Some campuses have long-standing services and include support groups for students. Some have services such as tutoring, resources for test accommodations, and accessible housing. Most campuses have designated one or more persons responsible for students with disabilities. Students with disabilities who are interested in attending postsecondary institutions need to be taught how to access the services and how to seek out institutions that will meet their needs.

Postsecondary personnel view students as adults. Unlike the secondary school setting, monitoring and follow-up are rarely available in postsecondary institutions. This makes it even more vital that students with disabilities have the advocacy skills, motivation, and determination to survive in adult roles. The ability to use the community and its resources is essential. Support personnel in the postsecondary setting will provide a linkage for students to fulfill their needs, but students will be expected to carry out the necessary actions. Classroom, curriculum, and equipment modifications will be determined by a student with the help of the support personnel, but the student often has the primary responsibility to communicate those needs to the professor or instructor. The Department of Vocational Rehabilitation can be helpful in terms of funding equipment modifications or instructional devices for the student, so interagency coordination is as vital at the postsecondary level as it is at the secondary level.

Transition planning requires the collaboration of a myriad of support services to meet the needs of students with disabilities who are not involved with vocational and technical education or postsecondary educational settings. Each district should identify the services that might be needed by looking at all students (K–12) receiving special education services. The formation of a transition advisory committee with representatives from adult service agencies will assist a district in taking a proactive stance in developing necessary services. In rural areas, this committee might be a county-wide interagency committee to develop services.

Transition Planning and Interagency Cooperation

It is impossible for one individual or even two to put together a successful transition plan for any student. A joint, collaborative effort on the part of a number of individuals is required to put all of the components in place. The importance of collaborative and interagency planning is also recognized in the recent reauthorization of the Individuals with Disabilities Education Act (IDEA). This federal legislation requires that transition planning emphasize "interagency linkages" and "coordinated activities" that bring together all key parties for joint action.

Some communities and school districts have formalized this "interagency linkage" by forming a transition advisory committee (TAC). A TAC is a formally organized group that operates under established rules and serves as a sounding board for policies, procedures, innovation, and ideas. The historical purpose of advisory committees has been to make nonbinding suggestions to schools and adult programs and services to improve the quality of the services of the organization. Other basic purposes of the advisory committee have been (a) to solicit support from the business community; (b) to gain community support for the organization, school, or program through publicity; and (c) to provide a link between the community and the school or organization.

WHAT IS A TRANSITION ADVISORY COMMITTEE?

Transition advisory committees have been, and continue to be a critical component in systems change as well as a critical component in the design and implementation of individualized transition plans for students. Blalock (1996) suggested that most statewide change projects and model demonstration projects have found that in order to change existing service delivery models, systemic, multilevel approaches are necessary with community-level activities as the cornerstone. Team formation and team activities are crucial for real change in transition programs and occur most meaningfully at the local level (Blalock, 1996).

A TAC is much more than advisory in capacity. It is a decision-making committee that may function at the state, regional, or local community level. The TAC is made up of individuals of equal status who share a concern for persons with disabilities and a desire for active participation and cooperative planning to improve the functioning of systems and to address the transition needs of these individuals (Miller, La Follette, & Green, 1988). Perhaps a title more reflective of the function of a TAC would be a community interagency transition planning committee, coordination committee, or community transition team.

Several factors should be addressed in the establishment of a TAC. First, TAC members must develop a mission statement and plan of action including goals and objectives. Second, representatives of each community and area organization whose participation and cooperation is fundamental to improving the transition of young adults with disabilities should be asked to participate. Initial membership may include parents, students with disabilities, educators, and adult service providers in the areas of vocational instruction and support, living arrangements, transportation, postsecondary education, leisure and recreation, and financial support services. While the goal of the TAC should be to include representatives of all groups, a conscious effort should be made to keep the size of the group small enough so each member can actively contribute during each meeting. Initially, no more than 25 individuals should be invited to participate. Later, membership may be expanded. One of the most important factors in establishing a successful TAC is active participation of all members during meetings. Third, the decision makers of organizations should be invited to become members of the TAC. Having an organization's decision maker involved in the TAC will enhance the opportunity for rapid organizational change.

If the public school is the lead agency in establishing a TAC, educators will have the opportunity and responsibility to identify potential members to participate in the TAC. Several factors should be considered when identifying members of the TAC, including experience, enthusiasm, and open-mindedness, as well as willingness and ability to commit time to TAC meetings and activities. Finally, gender and racial balance should be considered, as well as consumer participation, when the TAC is organized. When individuals are invited to participate in the TAC a letter of invitation should be written to each prospective member and followed up with a phone call and verbal invitation to participate.

WHAT IS THE MEMBERSHIP OF THE TRANSITION ADVISORY COMMITTEE?

While each community may have a different set of adult service providers and some differences in adult services for persons with disabilities, the following is a list of key community members and organizations you may wish to involve in the TAC initially. These include:

- Community college representative.
- Department of Employment Services personnel.
- Department of Human Services representative.

- Division of Vocational Rehabilitation Services representative.
- Education administrators.
- Parents.
- Providers of leisure and recreation services for persons with disabilities.
- Rehabilitation personnel from supported employment and work activity centers.
- Residential service providers.
- Special education support personnel.
- Special educators.
- Student representatives.
- University representatives.
- Vocational-technical instructors.
- Workforce Investment Council members.

In most situations, it will be impossible to invite every organization that provides services to persons with disabilities in each of the areas listed. As a result, every attempt should be made to encourage TAC members to solicit information and opinions from similar organizations or facilities. As the TAC matures and its members learn to work together, more members may be added to the group. Other service providers and interested parties might include employers, advocacy groups, and administrators of area transportation systems. The final composition of each group will vary widely depending on the strengths and concerns of the specific geographical area.

WHAT ARE THE ACTIVITIES OF THE TRANSITION ADVISORY COMMITTEE?

A TAC can assume a leadership role in any number of activities relating to the transition of young adults with disabilities from school to adult life. The following is a list of potential activities or goals for a TAC:

- Provide a forum for educators and adult providers to share information and clarify agency roles regarding the types of services that are provided for persons with disabilities. This activity may act to minimize conflict and competition among agencies.
- Identify strengths and concerns in the collective adult service delivery systems. It is important to identify gaps in service delivery as well as potential areas where agency services overlap or are duplicated. The TAC can work to eliminate duplication and fill service gaps.
- Take a leadership role in the development and dissemination of a needs assessment instrument to identify the information base and perceived information needs of parents and students regarding the adult service system.

- Take a leadership role in developing and disseminating a needs assessment instrument to secondary special education teachers to find out their understanding of the adult service delivery system.

- Develop or modify a transition planning procedure to meet the needs of the local area.

- Participate in field testing a transition planning procedure.

- Collaborate on follow-up studies regarding the post-high-school status of graduates of special education programs.

- Develop a transition information manual for students, parents, and secondary special education teachers regarding services and support systems available to graduates of special education programs within the adult service sector.

- Exchange information with teacher education programs in state institutions of higher education to increase the knowledge of preservice students regarding community resources for persons with disabilities.

- Work to enhance public awareness of postsecondary services for persons with disabilities.

- Collaborate to increase public awareness of the underutilization of persons with disabilities in the workforce.

- Sponsor and participate in workshops for students, parents, and secondary special education teachers regarding transition-related issues.

- Work with cities in the region to include jobs for persons with disabilities as a requirement for businesses applying for monies through economic development programs.

- Examine the possibility of identifying adult providers as case managers for specific students with disabilities.

- Develop videotape presentations of local adult service providers reviewing services offered by those providers.

- Develop cooperative release-of-information forms to improve the speed and efficiency of information exchange regarding specific students.

- Develop interagency cooperative agreements to allow providers to share information regarding clients with disabilities more effectively.

- Address service delivery issues for students and graduates who are difficult to place with the use of cooperative release-of-information forms.

- Support members of the system of services for persons with disabilities through publicity and by drawing to the attention of businesses and the community the important contribution that this system makes to the economic well-being of the area.

- Explore the use of a shared computer system to collect data, reduce the possibility of duplicating services for specific clients, and increase communication regarding persons with disabilities.

Without well-established goals and cooperative effort, the TAC could become just another committee of limited usefulness as a vehicle for group change.

WHAT ARE SOME TIPS FOR THE TRANSITION ADVISORY COMMITTEE?

During the initial meetings of the TAC, it is important to support all the agencies and individuals present, yet be honest and direct in identifying strengths and concerns in the current service delivery system. One strategy is to review the strengths and concerns of your agency or school regarding the transition of young adults with disabilities from school to adult life. This represents an opportunity to establish an honest and open dialogue. Look for opportunities to share credit across agencies and focus on concerns that are specific to your organization. Model risk taking as an appropriate behavior at TAC meetings. Solicit constructive criticism of your organization, and brainstorm potential solutions. Remember, transition cannot work without collaborative effort, collaborative planning, and the honest exchange of information.

Group facilitation of TAC meetings is an important issue. Consider electing co-facilitators to act as chairperson and secretary for the committee. During the initial year, consider drawing one facilitator from the adult service continuum and one from education.

How often the TAC will meet is always a difficult decision. The TAC must meet often enough to generate excitement yet not so often as to be perceived as a burden. A monthly meeting may be appropriate for many groups. In most cases, large-group meetings should not be held more than every 3 weeks or less than every 6 weeks. Meetings should be held at a regular, prearranged time so members can establish a regular time on their monthly calendars.

TAC meetings should be long enough to be productive, yet short enough to be fast paced and interesting. Some suggest approximately 2 hours per meeting.

Subcommittees should be established to work on specific group projects. Distribute leadership of these subcommittees throughout TAC membership.

Be project oriented and establish yearly goals for reviewing and evaluating the production of the TAC. Evaluate progress toward group goals on at least a biannual basis.

Minutes of each meeting should be provided to all TAC members promptly within 2 weeks of the meeting. This correspondence can also be used to remind TAC members of the time and location of upcoming meetings. Include the agenda for the next meeting in the mailing of the minutes of the last meeting. The agenda should clearly address the topics that will be covered in the next meeting. The topics on the agenda should be diverse enough to interest all individuals on the TAC.

Consider varying the location of meetings, and give each member of the committee the opportunity to host the TAC. This provides a wonderful opportunity for the group to tour facilities and explore services. (It also distributes the cost of refreshments across the entire organization.)

Remember that decision making and planning by committee are a consensus-building process. The process is time intensive, and sufficient time must be allotted to preplanning to maximize the opportunity for success at each meeting.

One activity that should be considered by the TAC is to review case studies of specific students with special education needs to explore how the system is functioning to meet their needs. This can be considered a reality check. The review can act as a monitor of the effectiveness of organizations in meeting the goal of an effective transition planning process. Remember, individual students can be discussed only with the signed consent of the student and parent. Again, this is an excellent reason for a group release-of-information form for members of the TAC.

The TAC is a critical component for transition planning. It provides the forum for real communication among agencies. It provides the opportunity for collaborative planning and system change. Team efforts cannot be understated where transition planning is involved.

Program Evaluation and Follow-Up

Program evaluation may seem like a monumental task. Before undertaking it, it is important to understand why it is being done and what benefits it can provide. Smith and colleagues (1987) defined program evaluation as a "planned process of gathering and analyzing data to help make decisions less risky" (p. 1). If we do not know what works, how do we decide what programs to offer? Program evaluation must be practical. It must be designed to answer questions we have about our students and our programs. "Bigger" and "more data" are not always "better." More time should be spent defining the questions that need answers rather than in analyzing too much data gathered for unknown purposes. For example, if we wanted to know whether community-based instruction leads to productive employment after graduation, we would design procedures to gather data on the secondary curriculum of comparable students who had and did not have community-based instruction and contact them after graduation to determine their current employment status (follow-up). Another example might be to determine whether or not the secondary curriculum is related to the success of students with disabilities in a postsecondary environment (Missouri LINC, 1991).

Follow-up should not be confused with follow-along. *Follow-along* is a term frequently used to indicate to parents and educators that assistance and support services are needed throughout the entire transition process, whether in school, out in the community, or in the home environment. It is necessary to track and monitor students' progress each step of the way, by following them carefully, to ensure the skill acquisition needed for transition from school to work. In following the transition process, if it is determined that services that were disconnected need to be reinstated or other agencies need to be accessed, then follow-along would provide for the necessary reentry.

WHAT ARE THE BENEFITS OF PROGRAM EVALUATION?

Transition program evaluation can help determine the effectiveness of curriculum and discover the areas of adult needs that other community systems should address. For example, a follow-up study may indicate that students are productively employed, but that they have little or no access to or use of recreational facilities in the community. This information could be given to the community parks and recreation department to develop strategies for access by populations with special needs. If transportation is found to be a barrier, the city council might be made aware of this fact. The follow-up study might indicate that former students are having a difficult time finding or maintaining employment, and further investigation might imply that their social skills are inadequate. This finding would impact the secondary curriculum and suggest that the teaching of social skills needs to be stressed in various ways throughout the high school years (Missouri LINC, 1991).

Transition program evaluation can help determine needed program improvements. Evaluation helps to locate the strengths and weaknesses in the various components of the transition program. In the example just cited, the weakness was found in social skills instruction. Likewise, evaluation can pinpoint strengths. For example, during the follow-up to a community-based instruction program it might be found that students who participated in community-based instruction for 3 or more years tended to be employed in full-time, competitive employment at a much higher rate than those who did not participate or who participated for a shorter time period. This finding would surely indicate a strong program component that might benefit more students if instituted in a systematic manner.

Program evaluation can also determine the necessity for program expansion. It can help identify areas of new needs and clarify the direction for expanding programs. An example might be the need for the inclusion of social skills instruction in the curriculum or the need to develop a parent involvement program.

Evaluation results can be used as a marketing tool. If distributed thoughtfully, the results can be used to gain understanding and support for the transition program in the school and the community. Positive findings, presented clearly, will help others see the relationship between the program and the successful outcomes of former students. Cost-effectiveness indexes might be used to demonstrate the efficiency of the program. For example, a chart could indicate the cost to society of having people on support programs (SSI, welfare) as opposed to the cost of appropriate education, postschool employment, and independent living.

Program evaluation can be a complex and confusing process. Probably the most difficult step is deciding where to begin. Assessing program effectiveness can be accomplished at various levels. One level is evaluation of individual outcomes, such as the increase in the use of appropriate social skills for a student whose IEP goals and objectives are written for this outcome. Another level is to evaluate a specific program component, such as the variety of jobs and satisfaction of students in a work/study program. The curriculum, another component of transition programs, could also be evaluated. These evaluations might be called *internal assessments*, since they rely on information generated within the school system.

External evaluations, so called because they entail obtaining information not necessarily found within the school itself, might include follow-up studies of school leavers; employer satisfaction with work/study students, or graduates; or surveys designed to discover parent satisfaction with their child's educational preparation. External evaluation may be more difficult to accomplish because it involves obtaining information from persons with whom school personnel have traditionally limited interactions (Missouri LINC, 1991).

West (1987) identified the following set of issues that need to be examined to determine the quality and effectiveness of programs:

- Administration of the program.
- Adequacy of staffing to meet program design.
- Coordination among regular, vocational, career, technical and special education.
- Identification of the target population the program intends to serve.
- Funding sources available to support the program.
- Purpose of the program.
- Curriculum content and appropriate course offerings.
- Resource and support services to supplement individual needs of the target populations.
- Comprehensiveness of support services.
- Assurances that legislative mandates are met. (p. 133)

Golin and Ducanis (1981) have suggested that to effectively evaluate programs operated by teams, it is important to identify a number of parties concerned with evaluation, such as, but not limited to:

- The student(s).
- The parent(s).
- The professional(s)/members of the team.
- The organization (in which the team operates).
- The taxpayers/employers/community. (p. 160)

What may seem to be an unqualified "good" or benefit for one may not be a benefit for others (Golin & Ducanis, 1981, p. 160). Many aspects can be evaluated: improvement in quality of life for the student, the cost effectiveness of transition, or the effectiveness of the transition services. Planning for transition program evaluation requires a long-term commitment to program evaluation.

WHY IS STUDENT FOLLOW-UP A NECESSARY PART OF TRANSITION?

Special education has assumed the responsibility of tracking students who leave the secondary school. Vital information is needed to design, improve, and/or revise transition services. These important data are collected by various methods, using multiple resources such as the following:

- Employment records of students.
- Promotion/advancement on the job.
- Awareness of postsecondary admissions.
- Feedback of services previously provided.
- Self-reporting of anticipated services in the future.
- Feedback from family members.
- Feedback from agencies still providing student services.
- Feedback from agencies regarding services requested and services provided.
- Polls of employers of students who have made the transition into the labor force.
- Polls of postsecondary representatives about the success of students enrolled in their programs.

This data analysis can be reported in various forms to the administration, parents, community, state education agencies, and adult service providers. Program evaluation is in large part a collection of pertinent information that documents services provided and student success. Legislation requires that data be collected to document progress toward student goals and objectives. Program evaluation is useless unless it is used to improve services within the delivery system. The following are examples of recommendations that could result from analysis of data collected:

1. Provide stronger links with employers through various advisory committees in order to determine industry labor market needs.

2. Provide stronger emphasis on postsecondary educational opportunities such as upgrading, retraining, career changes, and technological displacement.

3. Develop parent education programs to inform parents about the career development process and encourage them to become involved in the early stages to alleviate unrealistic expectations in job placement.

Once individuals with disabilities exit the educational system, specific follow-up data need to be collected and analyzed to facilitate the following:

- Documenting funding needs.
- Revising and updating curriculum.
- Designing delivery systems for transition services.
- Developing new resources and materials for IEP teams.

- Determining program priorities.
- Identifying transition services needing revision.
- Soliciting information from program consumers.
- Planning long-range transition services.

The transition process requires information from every component of the program. West (1987) contends that program evaluation determines whether or not the components, separately and together, have been effective. The results indicate to educators, families, and the community whether or not they have complied with legislative mandates, which includes abiding by the spirit as well as the letter of the law.

References

Association for Career and Technical Education. (1998). *The official guide to the Perkins Act of 1998.* Alexandria, VA: Author.

Barnes, A. (1991). *Facts about the Americans with Disabilities Act.* Unpublished monograph. Washington, DC.

Blalock, G. (1996). Community transition teams as the foundation for transition services for youth with learning disabilities. *Journal of Learning Disabilities, 9,* 148–159.

Boyer-Stephens, A., & Kearns, D. (1988). Functional curriculum for transition: Bringing relevance to the classroom. *The Journal of Vocational Special Needs Education, 11*(1), 13–18.

Brolin, D. E. (1982). *Vocational preparation of persons with handicaps.* Columbus, OH: Merrill.

Brolin, D. E. (Ed.). (1997). *Life-centered career education: A competency based approach* (5th ed.). Reston, VA: The Council for Exceptional Children.

Browder, D. M. (1987). *Assessment of individuals with severe handicaps: An applied behavior approach to life skills assessment.* Baltimore: Brookes.

Clark, G. M. (1990). *Functional curriculum strategies.* (Teacher training manual). Topeka: Kansas State Department of Education.

Cunanan, E., & Maddy-Bernstein, C. (1995). *Student services: Achieving success for all students.* Berkeley, CA: National Center for Research in Vocational Education.

Dougan, P. (Ed.). (1991). *Transition services language survival guide for California.* Sacramento: California Department of Education.

Edgar, E. (1987). Secondary programs for special education: Are many of them justifiable? *Exceptional Children, 53,* 264–270.

Golin, A. K., & Ducanis, A. J. (1981). *The interdisciplinary team: A handbook for the education of exceptional children.* Rockville, MD: Aspen.

Guerin, G. R., & Maier, A. S. (1983). *Informal assessment in education.* Palo Alto, CA: Mayfield.

Halpern, A. S. (1985). Transition: A look at the foundations. *Exceptional Children, 51,* 479–486.

Halpern, A. S., & Benz, M. R. (1987). A statewide examination of secondary special education for students with mild disabilities: Implications for the high school curriculum. *Exceptional Children, 54,* 122–129.

Halpern, A. S., & Fuhrer, M. J. (1984). *Functional assessment in rehabilitation.* Baltimore: Brookes.

Ianacone, R. N., & Stodden, R. A. (1985). Transition issues and directions for individuals who are mentally retarded. In *Transition issues and directions* (pp. 1–7). Reston, VA: Division on Mental Retardation, The Council for Exceptional Children.

Levinson, E. M. (1993). *Transdisciplinary vocational assessment: Issues in school-based programs.* Brandon, VT: Clinical Psychology.

Maxam, S. (Ed.). (1985). *Informal assessment: A handbook for LEAs serving special needs students in vocational education.* Columbia: Missouri LINC, Instructional Materials Lab.

Meers, G. D. (Ed.). (1987). *Handbook of vocational special needs education* (2nd ed.). Rockville, MD: Aspen.

Miller, R. J., La Follette, M., & Green, K. (1988). *Transition planning: Procedural manual and inservice training package* (Monograph). Cedar Rapids: Iowa Department of Education.

Missouri LINC. (1991). *The transition implementation guide.* Columbia, MO: Author.

Patton, J., & Blalock, G. (Eds.). (1996). *Transition and students with learning disabilities: Facilitating the movement from school to adult life* (pp. 213–235). Austin, TX: Pro-Ed.

Paulson, J., & O'Leary, E. (1991). *Developing and writing transition services within the IEP process.* Unpublished manuscript.

Rusch, F., & Chadsey-Rusch, J. (1985). Employment for persons with severe handicaps: Curriculum development and coordination of services. *Focus on Exceptional Children, 17*(9), 1–8.

Rusch, F., & DeStefano, L. (1989). Transition from school to work: Strategies for young adults with disabilities. *Interchange, 9*(3), 1–2.

Sarkees-Wircenski, M., & Scott, J. (1995). *Vocational special needs.* Homewood, IL: American Technical Publishers.

Sergent, M. T., Carter, R. T., Sedlacek, W. E., & Scales, W. R. (1988, Fall). A five-year analysis of disabled student services in higher education. *Journal of Postsecondary Education and Disability 6*(4), 21–27.

Shoultz, D., Dell, S., Skold, M., & Sorenson, J. (1991). *A shared vision.* Washington, DC.: U.S. Department of Education. (ED 362 220)

Smith, C., & Goodwill Industries of America, Inc. (1987). *Program evaluation: A self-study manual.* Menomonie, WI: Materials Development Center.

Stodden, R. A., Ianacone, R. N., Boone, R. M., & Bisconer, S. W. (1987). *Curriculum-based vocational assessment: A guide for addressing youth with special needs.* Honolulu: International Education.

Texas Education Agency Clearinghouse. (1993). Teaching tips for at-risk youth. Austin, TX: Author.

Van Reusen, A. K., Bos, C. S., Schumaker, J. B., & Deshler, D. D. (1994). *The self-advocacy strategy for education and transition planning.* Lawrence, KS: Edge.

West, L. (1987). Designing vocational programs for special needs individuals. In G. Meers (Ed.), *Handbook of vocational special needs education* (2nd ed., pp. 15–135). Rockville, MD: Aspen.

A Suggested Process
for Transition Planning

BEFORE THE IEP MEETING

1. Assist students and families to determine needs, preferences, and interests related to life after high school. Teach them to actively participate in the IEP meeting. Assess student needs, preferences, and interests.

2. Formally invite the student to participate in the IEP process and meeting.

3. Provide written notice of the IEP meeting to parents, students, and outside agencies.

4. If the student chooses not to attend the IEP meeting, use other means to gather information about his or her needs, interests, and preferences.

5. If an invited agency chooses not to attend the IEP meeting, use other means to ensure they participate in the planning of transition services. Document these efforts and include them in the IEP.

DURING THE IEP MEETING

6. Conduct the IEP meeting to actively involve the student and family. Review the student's present level of performance, needs, interests, and preferences, in order to guide the development of the following:

   - an outcome-oriented post-school vision and goals for education, employment, and living;

   - a statement of transition service needs at age 14 and every year thereafter focusing on the courses the student will need to study;

Note. From Storms, J., De Stefano, L., & O'Leary, E. (1996) *Individuals with Disabilities Education Act: Transition Requirements. A Guide for States, Districts, Schools and Families.* Reprinted with permission.

- coordinated activities in instruction, related services, community experiences, employment, and other post-school living objectives needed to achieve the post-school outcomes;

- daily living skills activities and a functional vocational evaluation, if appropriate;

- annual goals and objectives for coordinated activities that are the responsibility of the school; and

- identification of who will provide and/or pay for the above.

AFTER THE IEP MEETING

7. Provide the instruction, experiences, and services outlined in the IEP.

8. Conduct follow-up activities to determine if the transition services are provided as planned.

9. Reconvene the IEP team to plan alternative strategies if the transition services are not provided as planned.

Appendix B

Sample Statements, Goals, and Objectives

POSTSECONDARY EDUCATION/TRAINING

GOAL: With consultation from the guidance counselor at school, the student will participate in applied technology courses that support his/her postsecondary education plans.

Student will:

- Shadow in ATE (Applied Technology Education) or ATC (Applied Technology Center) program for two days.

- Participate in high school welding program.

- Attend electronic class at ATC on dual credit program.

- Tour three or four state ATCs.

- Identify two ATC programs, arrange tours and interviews with instructors.

- Identify ATC programs which meet her/his needs.

- Take ASVAB (Armed Services Vocational Assessment Battery).

GOAL: Identify preferred community college.

Student will:

- Complete and submit financial aid packet.

- Contact Career Center to determine support options and how they meet his/her needs.

Note. Adapted from *The IDEA of Transition A Teacher's Transition Handbook.* Utah State Office of Education Study Project, 350 East 500 South, Salt Lake City, UT, 84111. March 1995. Pp. 3–7. Reprinted with permission.

- Work with counselor or instructor to determine credits toward graduation and entrance to college.
- Contact and visit college of choice.
- Review three postsecondary catalogs.
- Take SAT or ACT.

ASSESSMENT

GOAL: With guidance counselor at school, student will complete assessments to determine his/her employment and vocational strengths, weaknesses.

Student will:

- Complete vocational assessment given by Job Service or other service provider.
- Complete an interest inventory.
- Self-assess employment/vocational abilities and interest after completing work samples.
- Shadow in an Applied Technology Center or business and assess necessary skills.
- Collect assessment data.

Parent will:

- Complete parent futures planning questionnaire and skill assessments.
- List and prioritize student's strengths and interests.

FINANCIAL

GOAL: Identify financial assistance needs to attend ATC.

Student will:

- Apply for Pell Grant.
- Call identified financial resources to determine eligibility requirements.
- Apply for SSI (Social Security Income) if appropriate.
- Make application to Vocational Rehabilitation and complete intake process.

LEGAL

GOAL: Identify several (simulated) legal problems in Transition Class.

Student will:

- Determine legal needs.
- Determine legal resources available in the community.

- Research legal resources.
- Simulate application for appropriate legal assistance.
- Apply for appropriate legal assistance, if a real problem exists.

Parent will:
- Contact attorney to determine possibility of setting up a trust.
- Contact attorney to determine appropriate estate planning options.
- Contact attorney for consideration of guardianship if student is likely to benefit from such action.

RECREATION/LEISURE

GOAL: Become aware of community recreation/leisure programs or activities.

Student will:
- Identify local recreation options.
- Visit/contact three recreation options.
- Evaluate recreation/leisure options of interest.
- Participate in one identified area of interest.
- Explore school activities/sports.
- Attend school dance.

TRANSPORTATION

GOAL: Increase his/her options to travel independently in the community.

Student will:
- Complete Driver Education training and obtain driver license.
- Find co-worker with whom to ride.
- Compare cost/purchase liability insurance.
- Call local/regional transportation company to determine services and costs.
- Explore transportation options (cost, hours, restrictions, routes).
- Practice riding public transportation.
- Purchase a car.

SOCIAL/RELATIONSHIPS

GOAL: Improve social and interpersonal skills with peers, co-workers, and family members.

Student will:

- Participate in mentor program.
- Demonstrate appropriate co-worker skills.
- Demonstrate appropriate dating skills.
- Demonstrate improved family relationship skills.
- Determine counseling/support needs.
- Determine appropriate community resources to meet counseling/support needs.
- Contact and interview potential professionals or groups to determine suitability to individual need.

MEDICAL

GOAL: Become aware of and obtain medical supports and assistance.

Student will:

- Identify helping professionals in medical field.
- Contact/locate medical assistance agencies in area of need.
- Apply for Medicaid or other appropriate medical resources in the community.
- Determine medical needs.
- Determine appropriate questions to ask medical professional.
- Call medical professionals to compare services and cost.
- Visit/research community health services.
- Design a file with all pertinent medical information.

FUNCTIONAL ACADEMICS

GOAL: Identify functional activities that require application of academic concepts in Transition Class.

Student will:

- Demonstrate functional math and employment related math skills.
- Demonstrate accurate use of calculator in class and in community settings.
- Determine personal learning and working style.

Appendix C

Suggested Transition Activities

The following lists from Fairfax County (Virginia) Public Schools' Transition Planning Manual can be used as a resource for students, parents, and teachers in developing appropriate transition plans.

CAREER ACTIVITIES

- Complete inventories assessing career interests and experiences.
- Compile a career exploration notebook.
- Participate in career-related courses, i.e., Teen Living, Technology Education, Keyboarding.
- Participate in Professional Technical Studies, i.e., Auto Technology, Cosmetology, Marketing.
- Participate in vocational, career, and technical education courses, i.e., Office Technology, Work Awareness and Transition, Building Maintenance, Special Center component.
- Investigate the career center.
- Participate in a volunteer experience.
- Participate in guidance-sponsored career day.
- Investigate career options through the career center.
- Participate in a career exploration unit.
- Observe people working in different occupations in the local community.
- Interview people working in different occupations in the local community.
- Job shadow employee at business site.
- Identify and understand occupational safety issues.

Note. From Fairfax County Public Schools, Fairfax, VA. (1998). Suggested Transition Activities. *Transition Planning Manual.* Reprinted with permission.

- Obtain a work permit.
- Participate in a part-time job.
- Participate in school-based work experience.
- Participate in community-based work training program.
- Explore job qualifications/requirements for job of choice.
- Use the job resource network, i.e., people, newspaper, career center, job fairs.
- Complete a job application.
- Develop a resume.
- Practice interviewing.
- Interview for a job.
- Research college entrance requirements.
- Attend college fairs and presentations by speakers at schools.
- Prepare for and take college entrance exams.
- Complete college applications.
- Explore supported employment options with local vendors.
- Develop a plan with Department of Rehabilitative Services counselor/Community Services Board case manager.

SELF-ADVOCACY ACTIVITIES

- Participate in the IEP/ITP meeting.
- Participate in developing ITP.
- Share ITP information with teachers.
- Use eye contact and appropriate body language.
- Use problem-solving strategies, i.e., recognize nature of a problem, develop and evaluate alternatives, anticipate consequences.
- Demonstrate independence, i.e., call in sick to school or employment.
- Communicate feelings.
- Share strengths and limitations related to disabilities and adaptations or accommodations needed to be successful, i.e., tape record lectures, assistance with note taking, written directions.
- Know the difference between assertive and aggressive behavior.
- Know current legislation as it pertains to education and employment.
- Accept responsibility for actions; admit mistakes.
- Acknowledge accomplishments and share them.
- Deal appropriately with problems on the job.

- Attend parent and student workshops about college, employment, postsecondary services, advocacy rights groups.
- Explore support services available at colleges of interest.
- School completers obtain school records.
- Identify personal learning style.
- Seek assistance when needed.
- Communicate medical needs.
- Identify mentor in the work setting.
- Utilize job coach services.
- Explore advancement opportunities at the job.
- Relay school information to parents.
- Create a personal profile sheet explaining disability and accommodation needs.
- Participate in writing weekly goals for the classroom.
- Self-evaluate and discuss progress.
- Contact and make appointment with Department of Rehabilitative Services counselor/Community Services Board case manager.
- Participate in class discussions as a member as well as a leader.
- Explore and participate in community advocacy groups.
- Take responsibility for homework assignments.
- Maintain an assignment book and an activities calendar.
- Explore social security benefits and options.
- Develop and maintain appropriate peer support network.
- Participate in disability awareness presentations and panels to school and community groups.

INTERPERSONAL/SOCIAL ACTIVITIES

- Write a thank you note.
- Write a letter to a friend or family member.
- Maintain appropriate social distance during conversations.
- Use appropriate voice volume during conversations.
- Maintain eye contact.
- Greet peers and adults appropriately.
- Use appropriate facial gestures.
- Seek attention and help using appropriate behavior.
- Participate in mentor program.

- Discuss problems and concerns.
- Participate in class discussions.
- Accept change of routine.
- Follow instructions in school/work environment.
- Express anger in an appropriate manner.
- Exhibit self-control when frustrated.
- Use appropriate behavior in confrontational situations.
- Interact appropriately with peers.
- Work with others in small group settings.
- Cooperate with teachers and administrators.
- Participate in extracurricular activities with peers.
- Participate in group counseling sessions.
- Listen and respond appropriately.
- Assist peers with assignments.
- Refrain from teasing others.
- Identify strategies for dealing with interpersonal conflict.
- Make positive statements about self.
- Make positive statements about others.
- Critique self and identify areas of improvement.
- Develop skills to disagree in an effective manner.
- Accept multicultural differences.
- Accept help when offered.
- Practice speaking in front of groups.
- Initiate conversation with others.
- Express opinions appropriately.
- Use please and thank you.

INDEPENDENT LIVING ACTIVITIES

- Understand/identify survival vocabulary/signs.
- Use the telephone book.
- Read labels and directions.
- Use the classified section of the newspaper.
- Read and order from menus.
- Dress appropriately for a variety of activities.
- Learn to do own laundry.

- Keep hair clean and brushed.
- Shower after physical education class.
- Understand basic nutrition needs.
- Use a shopping list for food purchases.
- Determine best food buys.
- Prepare own bag lunch.
- Demonstrate appropriate table manners.
- Purchase personal items from store.
- Determine shopping needs based on finances and lifestyle.
- Determine best product value.
- Identify home owning/renting expenses.
- Identify public transportation alternatives.
- Learn rules and procedures regarding public transportation.
- Use public transportation.
- Recognize need for basic health care.
- Identify basic health care facilities.
- Understand health insurance benefits.
- Understand workmen's compensation benefits.
- Identify different methods of payment.
- Open a checking account/savings account.
- Make change up to a dollar.
- Consistently bring money for lunch.
- Set up a weekly budget.
- Balance a checkbook.
- Prepare tax forms.
- Identify personal leisure needs.
- Identify and request information about community recreation programs.
- Initiate a leisure activity.
- Participate in extracurricular activity.
- Register to vote.
- Register at the draft board.
- Understand the governmental structure.
- Organize weekly calendar.
- Complete assignments on time.
- Use watch to follow daily schedule.

- Prioritize personal goals.

- Establish morning routine.

- Participate in driver's education course.

- Participate in family life program.

- Respond to emergency situations.

- Enroll in course such as Teen Living, International Foods.

Appendix D

Sample IEP Form

LIFE CENTERED CAREER EDUCATION
INDIVIDUALIZED EDUCATION PROGRAM FORM
(Use attachments as needed for each student)

Student Name: _____ School: _____ Grade: _____ Date: _____

SECTION I: Present Level of Educational Performance

SECTION II: Annual Goals
A. Academic Goals (see attachment)
B. LCCE Functional Skills for Transition Preparation (check those that apply)
This student will progress toward acquiring functional behaviors in the following competency areas. (Check the appropriate annual goals.)

____ 1. Managing Personal Finances	____ 12. Achieving Socially Responsible Behavior
____ 2. Selecting and Managing a Household	____ 13. Maintaining Good Interpersonal Skills
____ 3. Caring for Personal Needs	____ 14. Achieving Independence
____ 4. Raising Children and Meeting Marriage Responsibilities	____ 15. Making Adequate Decisions
____ 5. Buying, Preparing, and Consuming Food	____ 16. Communicating with Others
____ 6. Buying and Caring for Clothing	____ 17. Knowing and Exploring Occupational Possibilities
____ 7. Exhibiting Responsible Citizenship	____ 18. Selecting and Planning Occupational Choices
____ 8. Utilizing Recreational Facilities and Engaging in Leisure	____ 19. Exhibiting Appropriate Work Habits and Behaviors
____ 9. Getting Around the Community	____ 20. Seeking, Securing, and Maintaining Employment
____ 10. Achieving Self-Awareness	____ 21. Exhibiting Sufficient Physical–Manual Skills
____ 11. Acquiring Self-Confidence	____ 22. Obtaining Specific Occupational Skills

C. Other Transitional/Support Services Goals (check those that apply)

____ 1. Financial Assistance/Income Support	____ 5. Transporation
____ 2. Advocacy Legal Services	____ 6. Other _____
____ 3. Medical	____ 7. Other _____
____ 4. Insurance	____ 8. Other _____

SECTION III: Specific Educational Services Needed

Goal & Subcomp. Numbers	Special Services Needed	Special Media/Materials and Equipment	Individual Implementors

LIFE CENTERED CAREER EDUCATION
INDIVIDUALIZED EDUCATION PROGRAM FORM

SECTION IV: Short-Term Individual Objectives

A. Academic Goals (see attachment)

B. LCCE Functional Skills for Transition Preparation (check those that apply)

____ 1. Identify Money and Make Correct Change (1)
____ 2. Make Responsible Expenditures (1)
____ 3. Keep Basic Financial Records (1)
____ 4. Calculate and Pay Taxes (1)
____ 5. Use Credit Responsibly (1)
____ 6. Use Banking Services (1)
____ 7. Maintain Home Exterior/Interior (2)
____ 8. Use Basic Appliances and Tools (2)
____ 9. Select Adequate Housing (2)
____ 10. Set Up Household (2)
____ 11. Maintain Home Grounds (2)
____ 12. Demonstrate Knowledge of Physical Fitness, Nutrition, and Weight (3)
____ 13. Exhibit Proper Grooming and Hygiene (3)
____ 14. Dress Appropriately (3)
____ 15. Demonstrate Knowledge of Common Illness, Prevention, and Treatment (3)
____ 16. Practice Personal Safety (3)
____ 17. Demonstrate Physical Care for Raising Children (4)
____ 18. Know Psychological Aspects of Raising Children (4)
____ 19. Demonstrate Marriage Responsibilities (4)
____ 20. Purchase Food (5)
____ 21. Clean Food Preparation Areas (5)
____ 22. Store Food (5)
____ 23. Prepare Meals (5)
____ 24. Demonstrate Appropriate Eating Habits (5)
____ 25. Plan and Eat Balanced Meals (5)
____ 26. Wash/Clean Clothing (6)
____ 27. Purchase Clothing (6)
____ 28. Iron, Mend, and Store Clothing (6)
____ 29. Demonstrate Knowledge of Civil Rights and Responsibilities (7)
____ 30. Know Nature of Local, State, and Federal Governments (7)
____ 31. Demonstrate Knowledge of the Law and Ability to Follow the Law (7)
____ 32. Demonstrate Knowledge of Citizen Rights and Responsibilities (7)
____ 33. Demonstrate Knowledge of Available Community Resources (8)
____ 34. Choose and Plan Activities (8)
____ 35. Demonstrate Knowledge of the Value of Recreation (8)
____ 36. Engage in Group and Individual Activities (8)
____ 37. Plan Vacation Time (8)
____ 38. Demonstrate Knowledge of Traffic Rules and Safety (9)
____ 39. Demonstrate Knowledge and Use of Various Means of Transportation (9)
____ 40. Find Way Around the Community (9)
____ 41. Drive a Car (9)
____ 42. Identify Physical and Psychological Needs (10)
____ 43. Identify Interests and Abilities (10)
____ 44. Identify Emotions (10)
____ 45. Demonstrate Knowledge of Physical Self (10)
____ 46. Express Feelings of Self-Worth (11)
____ 47. Describe Others' Perception of Self (11)
____ 48. Accept and Give Praise (11)
____ 49. Accept and Give Criticism (11)
____ 50. Develop Confidence in Oneself (11)
____ 51. Demonstrate Respect for the Rights and Properties of Others (12)
____ 52. Recognize Authority and Follow Instructions (12)
____ 53. Demonstrate Appropriate Behavior in Public Places (12)
____ 54. Know Important Character Traits (12)
____ 55. Recognize Personal Roles (12)
____ 56. Demonstrate Listening and Responding Skills (13)
____ 57. Establish and Maintain Close Relationships (13)
____ 58. Make and Maintain Friendships (13)
____ 59. Strive Toward Self-Actualization (14)
____ 60. Demonstrate Self-Organization (14)
____ 61. Demonstrate Awareness of How One's Behavior Affects Others (14)
____ 62. Locate and Utilize Sources of Assistance (15)
____ 63. Anticipate Consequences (15)
____ 64. Develop and Evaluate Alternatives (15)
____ 65. Recognize Nature of a Problem (15)
____ 66. Develop Goal-Seeking Behavior (15)
____ 67. Recognize and Respond to Emergency Situations (16)
____ 68. Communicate with Understanding (16)
____ 69. Know Subtleties of Communication (16)
____ 70. Identify Remunerative Aspects of Work (17)
____ 71. Locate Sources of Occupational and Training Information (17)
____ 72. Identify Personal Values Met Through Work (17)
____ 73. Identify Societal Values Met Through Work (17)
____ 74. Classify Jobs into Occupational Categories (17)
____ 75. Investigate Local Occupational and Training Opportunities (17)
____ 76. Make Realistic Occupational Choices (18)
____ 77. Identify Requirements of Appropriate and Available Jobs (18)

LIFE CENTERED CAREER EDUCATION
INDIVIDUALIZED EDUCATION PROGRAM FORM

____ 78. Identify Occupational Aptitudes (18)	____ 89. Apply for a Job (20)
____ 79. Identify Major Occupational Interests (18)	____ 90. Interview for a Job (20)
____ 80. Identify Major Occupational Needs (18)	____ 91. Know How to Maintain Post-School Occupational Adjustment (20)
____ 81. Follow Directions and Observe Regulations (19)	
____ 82. Recognize Importance of Attendance and Punctuality (19)	____ 92. Demonstrate Knowledge of Competitive Standards (20)
____ 83. Recognize Importance of Supervision (19)	____ 93. Know How to Adjust to Changes in Employment (20)
____ 84. Demonstrate Knowledge of Occupational Safety (19)	____ 94. Demonstrate Stamina and Endurance (21)
____ 85. Work with Others (19)	____ 95. Demonstrate Satisfactory Balance and Coordination (21)
____ 86. Meet Demands for Quality Work (19)	
____ 87. Work at a Satisfactory Rate (19)	____ 96. Demonstrate Manual Dexterity (21)
____ 88. Search for a Job (20)	____ 97. Demonstrate Sensory Discrimination (21)

C. Other Transitional/Support Services Objectives (see attachment)

SECTION V: Date and Length of Time relative to specific educational services needed for this student

Goal Number	Beginning Date	Ending Date	Goal Number	Beginning Date	Ending Date

SECTION VI: Description of Extent to which this student will participate in the regular educational program

	Percentage of Time	Narrative Description/Reaction
Language arts	_____ %	
Math	_____ %	
Science	_____ %	
Social science	_____ %	
Vocational (Bus.) & Work Study	_____ %	
Physical education	_____ %	
(other) _____	_____ %	
(other) _____	_____ %	

LIFE CENTERED CAREER EDUCATION
INDIVIDUALIZED EDUCATION PROGRAM FORM

SECTION VII: Justification for type of educational placement of this student

Narrative Description/Reaction

SECTION VIII: Individual Responsible for implementing the individualized education program and transitional services

Name   *Role/Responsibility*

SECTION IX: Objective Criteria, Evaluation Procedures, and Schedule for assessing short-term objectives

Objective Criteria can be found in the LCCE Competency Rating Scale (CRS), the LCCE Knowledge Battery (KB), and the LCCE Performance Battery (PB). Criteria listed reflect the short-term individual objectives checked in Section IV, Part B, of this form.

Evaluation Procedures can be determined by the IEP Committee reviewing the manuals for the Competency Rating Scale, Knowledge Battery, and Performance Battery.

Schedule for Assessment should include time, date, frequency, place, etc.

SECTION X: Estimated Date, Location, and Time for next IEP Committee Review Conference

CEC Teacher Resources

Integrating Transition Planning into the IEP Process, Second Edition

Lynda L. West, Stephanie Corbey, Arden Boyer-Stephens, Bonnie Jones, Robert J. Miller, Mickey Sarkees-Wircenski

Help students make a smooth transition from school to adult life by making sure the skills they need for successful employment, community involvement. postsecondary education, leisure pursuits, and self-advocacy will be written into their IEP. Explore ways schools, community service agencies, private organizations, and families can work together.

A joint publication of the Division of Career Development and Transition (DCDT) and CEC.

#P386S   1999   70 pp   ISBN 0-86586-329-6 $21.95   CEC Members $15.95

IEP Team Guide

The Council for Exceptional Children

A guide for special and general educators involved in the Individualized Education Program—IEP—planning team. Contains useful reference lists, charts, and checklists. Explains what federal law requires, provides practical advice for carrying out roles as IEP team members, and follows the process of developing and revising an IEP.

#P5274   1999   103 pp   ISBN 0-86586-319-9 $29.95   CEC Members $20.95

Assess for Success: Handbook on Transition Assessment

Patricia L. Sitlington, Deborah A. Neubert, Wynne Begun, RIchard C. Lombard, and Pamela J. Leconte

Helps the IEP team decide what to assess and how assessment data should be collected and used within the context of career development. Case studies illustrate how this concept applies to students with different levels of ability and different career visions. Provides strategies for assessing self-determination skills.

A joint publication of the Division of Career Development and Transition (DCDT) and CEC.

#P5155   1996   136 pp   ISBN 0-86586-281-8 $30   CEC Members $21

A Practical Guide for Teaching Self-Determination

Sharon Field, Jim Martin, Robert Miller, Michael Ward, and Michael Wehmeyer

This practitioner's guide is targeted to K-12 special educators. It addresses self-determination; assessment; relationships among career development, transition, and self-determination; methods, curricula, and materials; and transition planning. Also explores topics related to self-advocacy and empowerment.

A joint publication of the Division of Career Development and Transition (DCDT) and CEC.

#P5231   1997   208 pp   ISBN 0-86586-301-6 $39.95   CEC Members $27.50

Life Centered Career Education: A Competency Based Approach, Fifth Edition

Donn E. Brolin

The curriculum spelled out in this book is the foundation for life skills and transition education for thousands of young people each year. It organizes 21 priority competencies into subcompetencies and objectives, as well as supporting activities for school and community. Reproducible forms include a student competency rating scale for easy assessment and a sample IEP form.

#P180G   1997   175 pp   ISBN 0-86586-292-3 $30   CEC Members $21

Life Centered Career Education: Modified Curriculum for Individuals with Moderate Disabilities

Robert J. Loyd and Donn E. Brolin

This modified version of the LCCE curriculum provides practitioners with the same easy-to-use format of the original version, but with modifications to the life skills competencies suitable for students with moderate mental disabilities. Knowing how and when to seek assistance is a key concept taught. A Modified Competency Rating Scale (CRS-M) and modified IEP form are also included.

#P5194   1997   120 pp   ISBN 0-86586-293-1 $30   CEC Members $21

Prices may change without notice.

Send orders to: The Council for Exceptional Children
Dept. K90450, 1920 Association Drive, Reston, VA 20191-1589
1-888-232-7733   Visit our Web site at www.cec.sped.org